The Knitted Knight

Published in paperback in 2023 by Sixth Element Publishing
on behalf of Susan Bird

Sixth Element Publishing
Arthur Robinson House
13-14 The Green
Billingham
TS23 1EU
www.6epublishing.net

© Susan Bird 2023

ISBN 978-1-914170-45-4

British Library Cataloguing in Publication Data. A catalogue record for this book is available from the British Library.

All rights reserved. No part of this publication may be reproduced, stored in a retrieval system or transmitted, in any form or by any means, electronic, mechanical, photocopying, recording and/or otherwise without the prior written permission of the publishers. This book may not be lent, resold, hired out or disposed of by way of trade in any form, binding or cover other than that in which it is published without the prior written consent of the publishers.

Susan Bird asserts the moral right to be identified as the author of this work.

Printed in Great Britain.

The Knitted Knight

Written and illustrated by
Susan Bird

OTHER BOOKS BY SUSAN BIRD
Available from Amazon

Colin and Fran Play Outside In The Autumn
Colin and Fran Splash Outside In The Summer
Agatha MaCat

ABOUT SUSAN

Susan Bird lives with her husband, Trevor, and family in the North East of England. Out of the many things she does, some of her favourite pastimes are writing, drawing, painting, sometimes knitting, sometimes playing guitar but mostly, and, in a big way, practising and teaching T'ai Chi and Feng Shou Kung Fu.

Dedicated to the knitters who lovingly create things
which bring comfort, joy and fire the imaginations of children.
And to my Mum, Grandma and Nana... who did just that.

Chapter One
Love is Magic

"You've put a spell on that toy," said Thomas's Mum to his Nana who had finished knitting the toy knight four days after Thomas was born.

"From me to you, with love," Nana said as she placed the toy knight in Thomas's cot. There it stayed all day and all night. As soon as he could, baby Thomas held onto his knitted knight tightly, playing and shaking it about a lot.

Teething Thomas chewed the toy's hand or foot now and then. Little Thomas played with his toy in his cot, in his pram, and even at the changing of the nappy, he would not let go. At bath time, his knitted knight sat next to the taps, sometimes getting a bit soggy. If Thomas had a cold, his toy would get a bit snotty and he never left the house without it.

"Want Ighty! Want Ighty!" he'd demand, wriggling like mad in his pushchair until his toy was safely back his hands. Yes, 'Ighty' had to come to the doctors, dentist, nursery, infant school and his Nana and Granddad's.

His Nana half wondered if she might have put too much love into making the knight because, at bedtime, Thomas would hold 'Ighty' to his ear like they were talking to each other. Then he would fall asleep like magic.

By the time Thomas was in junior school, he had renamed his little friend 'Sir Gladforthe' and, even though his toy was now a bit scruffy with one frayed boot, Thomas still told him all about his day, at every bedtime and he still fell asleep like magic.

1

Chapter Two
The Heavy Stone

It was Saturday morning. Thomas lay on Granddad's lawn under the shade of the hazel tree watching the sky. Through the dark green leaves and brown twigs, he saw strings of cloud drifting by. His knitted knight lay beside him.

Today was hard. It was the first time he had visited his Nana and Granddad's house since she had 'passed away' six weeks ago. He had been told this fact and he and his knight had been to her funeral with Mum and Dad. It wasn't the same as when they'd buried his hamster Goldilocks in the garden. Everyone had cried and smiled and told him he was "a very brave boy" and how lovely it was that his new baby sister was "on her way". But Thomas didn't understand any of it, not really. He did remember that he'd eaten a lot of sticky toffee pudding, felt a bit sick and had stared at Auntie Marion's eyebrows which she'd pencilled in wonkily that morning.

So today when he opened the front door to his Grandparents' house, he was shocked at how different it felt. Then it struck him… his Nana was gone, the house was empty of her.

Without even a "Hello", Thomas barged his way past his Granddad and into the front room just in case. He stared at her chair. Empty, of course, except for her latest knitting project, left unfinished. Thomas ran into the garden, scared of his feelings. He wanted to shout louder than the sky. He missed her. He thought of all the Nana smiles and cuddles they'd shared, the custards she'd burnt. "On purpose," she'd said. He thought about the sweets they'd scoffed together at the pictures or when they'd cycled around the park, even when it was raining.

His heart ached like hot heavy lava. What should he do? He stared hard at the sky, willing himself not to cry or shout, but he did want to shout. Tears tickled his ears.

Chapter Three
Granddad

"Thomas?" said his Granddad. "There you are. I've been looking for you. What are you doing out here? No good out here on your own, son."

"But Granddad, Nana…"

"She's gone, lad. Come here, let's be sad together."

Thomas ran into his Granddad's arms.

"I know, I know, lad, it's hard to believe." Granddad held his grandson tightly. "Your Nana was a wonderful lady, she was. She loved you so very much."

"No! No, she didn't," Thomas blurted, pushing himself free. He started to shake.

"What? Of course she did, you know that, lad. She loved you," said Granddad.

"No, she didn't. She couldn't have or she wouldn't have, have left… not while I am still a boy." Thomas felt the heavy lava in his chest harden to stone.

"I hate her! I hate her!" he shouted.

His Granddad's face crumpled, those words hurt them both. Thomas stared down at his toy knight in his hand, then, without looking back, ran out of his Nana and Granddad's garden.

Chapter Four
Running where?

He ran and ran then ran some more. The knitted knight's legs and arms jiggled in Thomas's hand. Tears streamed down his face, mixing with his sweat. Thomas could taste the salt on his lips but did not stop to wipe his face, instead, he kept on running and the knight kept on jiggling.

He ran through the park, past houses, along street after street, reaching the edge of town where the houses gave way to open farm land. He trampled through a farmer's ripening wheat field then into the woods where he rested against a blackthorn tree, but only for less than a minute because he could feel the heaviness in his chest. So, on he ran, panting non-stop, charging through the woodland glades, snapping twigs underfoot. The sound of each cracking twig bounced from tree to tree like a ten gun salute times ten.

On the other side of the woods, across another field, Thomas flopped to the ground by a stream, where he lay catching his breath. He pushed his face into the cold water and drank, not thinking if the water was clean or not. He drank some more then rolled over onto his back, still clutching his knitted knight.

He gazed at the wide sky. The clouds looked pinkish yellow against the grey blue dusk of the evening. Was that a star twinkling? The sky seemed perfect to him in that moment, almost magical.

'Really lovely,' he thought, 'like a pretty postcard in a travel shop.'

Soon Thomas rolled onto his side and, gazing at his knitted knight, smiled. The knight seemed to stare back, smiling sort of. Thomas's eyelids grew heavy and then he slept.

Chapter Five
Thomas meets the Knight

Later, Thomas awoke in darkness. 'I must have been asleep for ages,' he thought to himself but couldn't remember why or how he got wherever he was. He tried to get his bearings. He could hear a stream nearby and remembered drinking from it. In the distance, he saw some lights… a campsite maybe?

"Feeling better, lad?" a deep voice said beside him.

Thomas turned to see a large, a very large in fact, grown up, size XXL knight, kneeling beside him! From what Thomas could make out in the moonlight, he was sort of knitted!

'Weird,' thought Thomas, noticing the glint of his armour in the moonlight.

"Ye know where thou art?"

Thomas shook his head, happy he wasn't on his own in the dark, even if he didn't know this knight.

'Weird,' thought Thomas, 'very weird.' He felt as if he had known this fellow all his life.

Chapter Six
Lovely Old Girl

Granddad, keeping at a distance, had tried to follow Thomas through the streets, estates, parks and fields but Thomas was very fast. He knew that once Thomas entered the dark woods, there was little chance of catching up with his grandson. Granddad started down the furrow his grandson had made through the farmer's golden wheat field. There on the other side of the track stood a grumpy, no, an angry looking farmer, with legs apart, arms folded.

"Get out of my field!" shouted the farmer.

"Sorry, sorry. Following my Grandson," Granddad explained, making his way towards the cross farmer. "He's very upset, he's lost his Nana, you see."

"His Nana, eh? Not seen no Nana round here?" said the farmer, still cross. "You and your grandson might damage my ripening wheat. That's good food, that is."

"No… my wife, the boy's Nana… well, she died just last month."

The farmer's face softened.

"First time he's visited since… since…" Granddad sputtered. "See. Ran off blindly. Sorry."

"Oh no, no. NO! I am so sorry to hear that," said the farmer, nodding slowly. "My condolences. A shock for the lad, then."

Granddad nodded as he trod, nearing the farmer. The farmer gazed across the pinkish golden field and confided, "I lost my Debra last week. Nothing would save her… no time."

"Oh, how dreadful, so sorry," Granddad muttered.

"Thank you." …*sniffle, sniffle*… "She was lovely, the old girl." …*sniffle, sniffle*… "She's left a big hole she has," said the farmer, his eyes filling with tears.

"I understand," said Granddad. "Melody and I had been married 34 years… I feel so empty."

"Eh? What? Oh! No, no." …*sniffle, sniffle*… "Debra was my prize pig. She fell through the rusty old cattle grid, a big hole she made, she did." Then the farmer burst into tears. "Such a lovely pig," he wailed and wailed.

Granddad's mouth fell open but thought it better to keep quiet. So he closed his mouth and pressed on.

Chapter Seven
Found Grandson

Granddad had lost valuable time tracking Thomas, so it was some time before he caught sight of something by a stream on the other side of the field, near to the farmer's campsite. There really was something… or someone. He hurried over. Yes, it was Thomas!

Granddad bent down and knelt beside him.

"Thomas? Thomas? Are you alright?"

Thomas didn't wake up.

"Thomas!"

Silence. Granddad checked his grandson's breathing. It was slow and steady. He checked to see if Thomas had any bumps, bruises, rashes or broken bones. Seemed okay. Then shaking him gently, he said, "Thomas, Thomas, wake up, lad. Can you hear me? Thomas?"

Nothing, Thomas didn't move at all. He seemed to be fast asleep. Granddad hadn't brought his mobile phone. Now he was very worried. It was way too far to carry the lad back home into town, so he carried him carefully over to the nearby campsite. Someone would surely have a phone and a blanket?

Chapter Eight
The Camp

Thomas and the knight crossed the lumpy ground towards the camp. The tents were mostly round, shaped like small circus tents. Too many to count, thought Thomas. As they neared the campsite, he could hear mumbling. The sounds of clanking metal, laughter and swords splicing through the air grew louder with every step. Suddenly a thrash of metal cut the air. A spearhead stopped less than a metre away from the knight's breastplate!

"Halt!" barked a voice in the dark. "State your business this night!"

The Knight frowned. "Do you not recognise me, guard?"

Thomas noted the stern tone the knight used.

There was a pause. The spear withdrew from the Knight, and a guard stepped into the moonlight. He wore a padded coat with a leather waistcoat over, no armour except a helmet made of dull metal and a sword in a leather scabbard hanging from a rope belt, Thomas noted. Oh and the spear!

"Sir Gladforthe? Forgive me, Sire. I did not recognise you," said the guard.

"No matter, you guard well. Take me to the Master of the Woods."

"My orders are that no stranger may enter the camp, Sire," the guard said, holding Thomas at the end of his spear.

"Come ye! I will vouch for the boy, he will not bring dishonour."

"But..."

"And I will tell the Master of the Woods that I commanded you to do as such," replied the Knight firmly.

"Very well, your Lordship." The guard raised his spear.

Sir Gladforthe strode into the camp.

Thomas trotted after... this was all very weird.

Chapter Nine
The Campsite

Granddad could hear the clanking of pots and pans, the opening or closing of tent zips and the murmur of voices.

"Stop! Who are you?" a young voice said in the dark, his torch shining in Granddad's eyes, making him squint.

"It's my Grandson, I can't wake him. Can you get help?"

"Mum, Mum. There's a man with a dead boy in his arms! I think he's a zombie!"

"Don't make up stories, Mathew! This isn't the telly!"

"No, Mam, really. There. Look!" He shone his torch on Thomas lying across his Granddad's arms.

"Please, help!" pleaded Granddad.

Mathew's Mum rushed over to help.

"Mathew! Fetch them a drink, will you? Thanks, love," said Mathew's Mum.

"I found him like this by the stream," said Granddad. "He's been running all afternoon."

"Is he hurt?" asked Mathew's Mum.

"I don't know. He might have drunk from the stream."

"Nah, it's spring water, it's okay," said Mathew's Dad.

"Poor little mite might just be worn out, that's all.

13

He'll wake up soon. I'll make you a nice cuppa and you can tell us all about…" said Mathew's Mum.

"Can I, can someone call a doctor? I've left my mobile at home," said Granddad.

"Of course." Mathew's Dad handed Granddad a tatty, battered old mobile phone, scratched with a cracked screen.

Granddad raised an eyebrow, thinking it was a piece of old junk.

"It works fine," said Mathew's Dad.

Chapter Ten
Master of the Woods

"What is this, bringing 'an unknown' into camp?" bellowed the Master.

Thomas hid a little behind the Knight.

"I can vouch for him. I have known him since he was a babe in arms. He is no threat, my Lord."

The Master of the Woods eyed the boy carefully for some time.

"Very well. Fetch me a drink, boy." He gestured towards a dull metal jug and goblets on a nearby table.

Thomas looked at Sir Gladforthe, who nodded. Thomas carefully poured the sweet smelling drink for the grownups from the heavy metal jug. He didn't dare ask to try some.

"Now, to business, Sir Gladforthe. State your piece."

"It's the boy, my Lord, he has lost something that cannot be replaced ever. But cannot tell us what it is."

"Is it an Oath that forbids him?"

"Nay, my Lord. I fear he has a spell upon him. The spell of muddled memory."

"Ah yes, I have heard of this spell. A spell, borne of great sadness."

'But I don't feel sad, just sort of heavy,' thought Thomas, wide-eyed.

"What will you do?" asked the Master.

"Alas, I know not," said Sir Gladforthe.

"Do you care for this boy, Sir Gladforthe?"

"Yes, my Lord, he is my ward."

"Then the path is clear. Both must quest to find the wise woman who can cure him mayhap. Be swift, Knight, ere the stone becomes set, then it will be too late."

Sir Gladforthe whispered to Thomas, "The stone will crumble, Thomas, do not worry."

'Cure, muddled memory? Stone? What stone? What path needed clearing? Too late for what, The Garden Centre? What on earth were these grownups going on about?' thought Thomas. 'That's grownups for you… always talking in riddles, so no point worrying.'

"And Sir Gladforthe, when you are done, there is a new position you must take, without question. Do not be long." And with that, the Master turned to consult a large map that seemed to be painted on a little, crusty, old tablecloth or some such like.

'Mum would go spare,' thought Thomas, 'if my Dad drew on our tablecloth.'

He glanced about for Mrs of the Woods? 'She'll be furious,' thought Thomas.

Sir Gladforthe bowed to the Master, nodding to Thomas to do the same.

"Follow me," he said.

Chapter Eleven
The Word Ward

"What's a ward, then?" Thomas asked, as he and the Knight strode towards some horses.

Sir Gladforthe was silent. Thomas wondered if he should address the Knight like he had heard on those old shows his Mum and Dad watched on the TV. He cleared his throat and began, "Dear Knight, I mean, Sir Gladforthe, err… pray tell me, Sir Knight, err… dust thou know the meaning of the word ward… err… for I have only been a reader of books for a very small number of years? Sir, err… for truth? Or soothe, is it?"

After what seemed like minutes rather than seconds… "Nae, lad. I do not know the meaning of *wordward*," Sir Gladforthe replied, half smiling.

"Not *wordward*, the word ward. What does it mean?" Thomas stressed, a little irritated.

"What does it mean 'Sir!'" commanded the Knight.

"Sir! Sorry Sir!"

'This was like talking to a schoolteacher,' thought Thomas, sulking.

"Forgive me, lad. I jest. A ward is a person or persons under my care, whom I protect until they can protect themselves."

"Like a Father and Mother?"

"More at a distance, like a tutor or god parent."

"Oh, I see," said Thomas, but he did not.

They rode on. Thomas didn't know why he was Sir Gladforthe's ward, nor did he know about this quest or why he could ride a horse so easily when he had only ever ridden a bike… and do stones set? Like hard, forever?

Chapter Twelve
The Doctor

"All his vitals seem to be fine, Dr Woods," said the ambulance driver. "Blood sugars are a little low but his granddad tells me he hasn't eaten since breakfast."

Doctor Woods examined the boy carefully. "Mmmmmm, unusual."

"You'll be okay, won't you, son?" said Granddad. "You'll come back to your Granddad. Your Mum and Dad will be wondering what you've been doing and there's your new baby sister to think about. Your Mum is due anytime now."

"I suspect, Mr Windsor, that your grandson is simply sleeping. We'll run some tests to be sure once we're at the hospital."

"I'd better ring my son and his wife."

"Here," said Mathew's Dad, offering Granddad the rather worse for wear mobile phone again.

Doctor Woods raised her eyebrows. "Perhaps you'd better accompany me to the hospital, Mr Windsor. I'll make the call to his parents."

Thomas's Granddad obeyed.

The campers watched the ambulance headlights disappear over the rise of the hill.

"Eeh, I wonder what the little mite is dreaming about?" said Mathew's Mum.

"Zombies," said Mathew.

Chapter Thirteen
What a Knight does and does not

Thomas and Sir Gladforthe rode many miles over mountains, through narrow valleys, across fields and through dry gorges formed by rivers thousands of years ago. Each night they camped in some sheltered spot selected by Sir Gladforthe, who seemed to know what he was doing.

Thomas's job was to gather wood for the fire whilst the Knight prepared the food caught that day, usually skinning a rabbit or gutting a fish. Thomas preferred not to look. It made him feel a bit squeamish. All the same, he ate the food as there was nothing else.

One evening, Thomas, while chewing on a bit of rabbit and three day old bread, happened upon the thought that he had been wearing the same clothes for twelve days. He was starting to feel a bit smelly, even by his standards.

"Sir Knight, pray inform me. My clothes are a bit smelly. Who is going to wash my clothes?" he asked hopefully of the knight.

"Smelly, you say? It cannot be. Why ye have only been wearing those clothes for a mere handful of days. Whereas I myself have been wearing this tunic for several months now."

Thomas had presumed the smell was the horses!

The Knight chuckled. "Wash your clothes? Hah! I will not wash your clothes, lad."

Thomas didn't mind having dirty clothes so much, but not smelly clothes… who would wash his clothes then? He wondered.

"Will I be able to have a bath soon?"

"A bath? A bath? Lad, do ye think ye a prince?" said the Knight, raising an eyebrow and laughing out loud. "A princely bath… Ye have some funny ideas, boy! A bath! Why you would have to travel all the way to Persia, my lad… and thy butt would indeed be sore! Ha ha ha!"

"No, not nobility, Sire, your ward. I just fancy a bath, that's all," replied Thomas, now not sure if he liked being a Knight's ward. "It would be nice, I thought. This saddle is a bit 'uncomfy' like."

"Do you find your saddle uncomfortable, lad?"

"Aye… I mean… yes, my Lord," said Thomas.

"Why I think perhaps ye are a prince, it has only been twelve days!" the Knight laughed. "Now, get ye some sleep now, lad. We are up early the morrow."

Thomas did as he was bade and settled down for the night on the heap of bracken they had each gathered. When the Knight covered him over with his blanket, Thomas soon slept.

Chapter Fourteen
Accident and Emergency

Thomas's Dad waited near the entrance of the hospital, pacing to and fro in front of the glass doors, only stopping when the ambulance workers rushed someone inside. At last they brought Thomas in on a wheeled stretcher.

"Thomas, Thomas. It's your Dad here," he said, keeping pace with the trolley as the ambulance workers pushed through two more sets of double doors.

Granddad followed.

"It'll be alright son. Your Dad's here," they both said.

The doctors examined Thomas, his breathing, ears, hands, feet and stomach. The nurses took his bloods and were busy rigging the young boy to an electrical machine that beeped. Beep… beep…. beep… beep… Thomas's Dad couldn't wait any longer.

"Will he be alright, Doctor? What's wrong with him?"

No answer. Then Thomas's Dad, angry with worry, shouted at Granddad, his own father!

"Sheena's having our baby now, right now! I should be with her! You were supposed to be looking after him, Dad!"

"Mr Windsor! We are running some tests to rule out a few things. We think he'll be okay. Your Dad found Thomas, carried him across a field to find help. Please calm down so we can work."

"Calm down, calm down? My wife is having a baby, my son is in some sort of coma and my Dad is looking terrible," shouted Thomas's Dad. "How can I calm down?"

"Son!" said Granddad sternly. "Please forgive him, Doctor Woods. He lost his mum, my wife, last month."

"Because, Mr Windsor," Doctor Woods said quietly, "you have no choice… your wife and family need you."

This quiet truth seemed to reach Thomas's Dad. He stood still and took some deep breaths, which helped to calm him.

"I am sorry, Doctor. I'm sorry, Dad. I miss Mum too."
"It'll be alright, son," said Granddad.

They hugged each other.

"Now go upstairs. Sheena needs her husband, there's a new baby coming into the world. I'll stay with Thomas. Go on."

Turning to the Doctor, Thomas's Dad said, "I'm really sorry for losing it a bit. Thank you."

"Go to your wife, Mr Windsor," said the Doctor, smiling.

Chapter Fifteen
Nuncheons

In the morning, Thomas found an extra blanket on top of his saddle. Thomas glanced over to the Knight.

"Thank you, Sir Gladforthe."

He nodded. "Mount your steed, lad."

They wandered on. Thomas wondered when they would finish this quest and when they would eat, having set off each morning without eating. That morning, they had been riding for at least three hours when Thomas finally plucked up the courage to ask a question.

"Why do we not have breakfast each morning?" he said.

"Break fast? What is break fast?" said the Knight.

"It's what you eat when you wake up in the morning," explained Thomas.

"Ah yes, you mean Nuncheons… before dinner."

"Nuncheons? Yes, well, sort of, only earlier, as soon as we get up the morning?"

"Mmmm. No, eating then would not be practical," Sir Gladforthe told him, explaining that they did not eat straightaway because (a) a fire would have to be lit to cook something and (b) they'd have to catch something. There simply wasn't the time. Sir Gladforthe told him if he wanted to get up earlier to collect the firewood and go hunting, he would eat this breakfast with him. Thomas didn't fancy that so he kept quiet. He didn't understand the life of a Knight.

They rode on in silence.

"Couldn't we catch something the night before and collect extra firewood then?" Thomas suggested hopefully.

"Wolves." the knight replied.

Chapter Sixteen
Swim for your supper

The sun was high, warming the day, when presently they came to a riverbank. Sir Gladforthe brought the horses to a halt.

"It's decided," said the Knight. "We will make camp here. But first we will swim, that's the nearest thing to a bath we'll get."

"But I've never swum in a river before, Sir Gladforthe," said Thomas, scrambling down from his horse.

"But you can swim?" said the Knight.

"Well, yes, a bit," replied Thomas.

"Come on then," said the Knight, "take your shoes off but leave your clothes on, they will wash while you swim."

The Knight dove into the river and Thomas jumped in after.

"Brr... the water's a bit cold, but I like it!" said Thomas, floating on his back. This part of being a Knight's ward was fun.

The Knight dove under the water. For a few moments, Thomas was almost worried until the Knight appeared right beside him.

They both swam and dove under the water, splashed and laughed.

"Let's fish. I'll teach thee," said the Knight. "Fetch my spears, lad."

They stood, knee deep in the water, spears in hands. "Be still, lad. Wait until the fish comes to thee."

They waited for what seemed like an age and then suddenly the Knight stabbed the water. He withdrew his spear, revealing a skewered large brown trout.

"There, as easy as that. Now, lad, catch thy own supper, ye be old enough!" And with that, the Knight leapt out of the water, leant the spear with the trout against a rock and began collecting wood. Soon Thomas could smell the juicy fish roasting over the fire. His mouth watered. He stabbed the water faster and faster and scared all the fish away.

"Be still, lad. Shadow behind you!" called the Knight.

Thomas turned around and waited, eyeing the water. He breathed slowly then moments later darted his spear into the water.

"I've got one! A fish!" cried Thomas, not quite believing his luck. "Look! Look! A fish! I've caught a fish!"

Sir Gladforthe smiled. "Aye, now, bring it over, young one. I'll show you how to rig a spit over the fire."

Thomas thought it was the tastiest fish he had ever eaten, ever.

Chapter Seventeen
Homeward

"This is your baby sister, Thomas. She's called Melody. It was your Grandma's name, lovely name that."

"We've run the necessary tests. Thomas is perfectly fine and it appears that the nurses have been able to feed him by guiding his hand over the food." The doctor paused, frowned and then continued. "It's strange that he feeds himself. Nurse Topper said he's been mumbling and nodding something, couldn't make out a word. But she did say he laughed out loud at one point. All good signs."

"Can we take him home with us, Doctor?" Thomas's Mum said hopefully. "We can look after him and the baby. Maybe… if he's surrounded by familiar sounds, he'll come back to us sooner?"

"Mmmm…. it might be too much for you," said the Doctor doubtfully. "He'll need washing, feeding, keeping warm and checking for bed sores three times daily, stretch his legs and arms. It's a lot with the new baby."

"We'd rather have him home, if we can," said Thomas's Dad.

"How about I take him home with me? Just for a few days, till you are settled," offered Granddad.

"That would be better, I think," said the Doctor, and then he turned to Granddad. "The dietician has recommended high protein foods. Nurse Baxter says he likes fish and chips and tuna."

"Rubbish!" said Thomas's Dad. "Tuna? Fish? What, our Thomas?"

"No. Thomas doesn't like fish," said both parents, in unison.

"Well, he does now," confirmed Nurse Baxter. "Yes, he's been stuffing his face with cod, haddock, even sardines. He's been chomping away like a hungry footballer!"

Thomas's parents frowned a bit, then looked at baby Melody, looked at Granddad then each other.

"Maybe just for a few days, then," said Thomas's Dad.

Chapter Eighteen
"Hush, Lad."

They had risen at the crack of dawn, following a track deep into an ancient forest. Thomas noticed there was little noise save the thump of their horse's hooves on the muddy path and the odd dull clunk of the Sir Gladforthe's armour.

"There's an Inn not far, only an hour's ride from here. We can fill our bel.... shhh!" He stopped the horses. "Do you hear it, boy?"

Thomas listened and could just make out a noise.

"Whaah, whaah, whaah."

"Do you hear it?"

"Yes. Yes, I do. I think it's coming from over there." Without a thought, Thomas slid down from his horse and ran towards the sound. In his hurry, he snapped twigs. The sharp cracks echoed through the forest.

"Shhh, lad! There are robbers on this road who'd take your horse. Slow down, it could be a trap!"

Thomas dropped swiftly onto his haunches and peeped through the hedgerow. He glanced back but Sir Gladforthe was gone. The horses? Gone.

Thomas felt fear strike through him. He was on his own! He waited under the shadow of a tree.

Chapter Nineteen
Robbers?

"Whaah, whaah!"

That sounds like a baby, thought Thomas. He was about to step out from his hiding place when he heard a thunder of galloping horses. He saw riders, six in leather, one wearing armour. All had swords, and the one in armour had a shield. They paused exactly where Thomas and Sir Gladforthe had just been. He wished he was by Sir Gladforthe's side right now. There was something he didn't like about those riders.

"They seem to have stopped here, my Lord," said one of the horsemen.

Thomas hoped the baby would keep quiet in case they turned and spotted him.

"They cannot be far away, we'll soon have them. Ride on!" commanded the Knight.

They rode off. Thomas watched the horse's hooves kicking up mud as the riders galloped into the distance. There was still no sign of Sir Gladforthe.

"Whaah, whaah, whaaah!"

Thomas turned to the job in hand. He kept as low as he could, darting from bush to tree trunk, doing his best to stay out of sight until he knew he was near whatever it was making that sound. He could see something up ahead… it was a basket and he could see a little foot sticking up now and then. It was a baby!

Where are its mum and dad? Thomas wondered. Surely they can hear it crying. He felt quite angry that a baby was left out here, on its own, with maybe robbers lurking nearby or wolves!

He decided to wait a while until he was sure it wasn't a trap or at least until the parents came back… or Sir Gladforthe, for that matter.

In the meantime, he looked about for wolves.

Chapter Twenty
Bears?

Grrrrrrrrrowl! Thomas's stomach echoed through the forest. He stifled a giggle. He imagined he was a bear hiding. But then he started to wonder about bears in the forest, bears that might be hungry, bears that might come and eat the baby. Or him! And the wolves! He wasn't sure about this quest business anymore.

"Whaaaah, whaah, whaah!"

"Shhhh, shhhhh," whispered Thomas, as loudly as he dared.

'I bet the baby is hungry too,' thought Thomas.

He thought about nuncheons then remembered to stay on his guard. He peered into the forest. He was scared for the baby.

The baby was quiet now. 'Probably asleep,' thought Thomas, but just to make sure, he thought he'd better have a quick peek, in case it was poorly. He looked hard into the woods surrounding the baby and then crept towards the basket. He had expected to see the baby asleep but it was not. Instead it was playing with its foot. When the baby saw Thomas, it smiled, eyes sparkling, and began waving its arms and legs about.

"Where's your mummy and daddy, little one?"

"Gurgle coo, coo gurgle," replied the baby.

Thomas carried the basket with said baby under the tree where it was shady and safer than on that rock. He could look after it until its mum and dad came back.

Thomas and the baby waited. He found a few bilberries that he squished into the baby's mouth. It wasn't much but it was something. He liked bilberries. He used to go bilberry picking with his... with his... with someone anyway. He sat with his back to the tree trunk, one hand on the basket. The only sound was a gentle whisper of leaves. Soon they were both snoozing.

Sir Gladforthe watched from afar.

Chapter Twenty-One
Sir Gladforthe

When the baby coughed a little, Thomas woke with a start. The light was fading and Thomas knew that the baby's parents weren't coming. He picked up the basket to head back to the path where he had left Sir Gladforthe. Wary not to be seen by wolves, bears or robbers, Thomas moved from bush to tree in the shadows until he saw what looked like Sir Gladforthe with both horses, right where he had last seen him. He approached cautiously just to be sure it was the right Knight and not some robber.

"There ye be, Thomas. What have ye there? Food, I hope!"

"No, it's a baby! And it's hungry too! Where did you go? "

"I hid when I heard the horsemen. Ye were nowhere to be seen. I was never far from ye."

"I was waiting for its mum and dad to come back."

"I know. Ye are brave," said the Knight.

"I waited for you!"

"Indeed. Now, mount thy steed! We cannot dally," commanded Sir Gladforthe.

"But, but…"

"Alas!" the Knight said loudly. "I fear that this baby is all alone. At the Inn, we'll buy food for us and the baby, perhaps learn of this child there." He passed the water horn to Thomas. "Here. Give it some water. Soon it will be twisting for food."

"I did feed it bilberries."

The Knight chuckled.

"Bilberries, eh? Aye, ye will change its napkin, me thinks."

They rode towards the Inn. Every now and then, the Knight would burst into laughter. Then he'd say, "Bilberries," and laugh all over again. Thomas had no idea why he was laughing but smiled anyway, happy to be back with his Knight.

Chapter Twenty-Two
The Inn

As luck would have it, the Innkeeper kept some goats for milk, cheese and meat.

"It's what my two were fed," said the Innkeeper. "Take a seat. I'll bring ye your food. Our lass will bring the babbie milk, warm and fresh from the udder."

'Urgh! Udder milk. 'Gross!' thought Thomas.

They sat on the crude bench outside the Inn, basking in the afternoon sun. The baby started to cry.

'It's the smell of food,' thought Thomas as his stomach rumbled and growled again.

The Innkeeper's wife brought a funny little cup thing over to their table

"I've put the milk in this here pot beaker with a spout. She'll get the hang of it."

"How do you know it's a girl?" Thomas demanded, too hungry to say 'thank you'.

"Thank ye, my Lady!" Sir Gladforthe corrected Thomas. "Forgive my ward, dear lady, for we have travelled far. We happened upon this baby in the woods. Thomas here waited all day for its mother and father, but alas, they did not show. We have not eaten this day."

"Well then, your Lordship. I best fetch ye thy food and make enquiries."

"Thank ye, we shall wait."

Thomas carefully dripped the milk into the baby's mouth. She guzzled it down, burped and then giggled. Soon some stew, bread, cheese, apple and ale arrived. They both ate heartily. Mmmm, this was really tasty. As they finished their last mouthful, the little baby started to wriggle then squashed its face up for a few moments, clenching its little fists and toes. Thomas giggled.

Then she sort of grunted a bit and nearly went cross-eyed. Thomas thought this baby very funny and very strange.

'What's it doing?' he wondered… that is until a distinct whiff of poo, tinted with acidy smelling bilberry, reached his nose. Thomas picked the baby up. "Urgh! You're smelly!" The baby smiled sweetly. Thomas found it hard to accept that a baby so cute could make such a stink so foul. Sir Gladforthe, for some reason, had already left the table and entered the Inn.

"Sir Gladforthe, wait…"

Chapter Twenty-Three
The Napkin

Heads turned when Thomas and the stinky baby wafted into the Inn. Everyone was watching them. The Innkeeper frowned but Thomas took no notice of their glares as he stomped over to Sir Gladforthe.

"Here, to thank ye for thy kindness." Sir Gladforthe placed a few lumpy coins in the Innkeeper's hand.

"Ye be welcome, Sire. Tis but the least we can do."

"Excuse me, Sire," said Thomas, "but, the baby needs changing."

"Indeed. The landlady has put all ye need in the attic. Ye did feed it bilberries…"

"But I don't know how, Sire. Please…" said Thomas

"Tis simple lad, use thine eyes. Now, there be the stairs," said the Knight, firmly guiding Thomas and the baby past the all glaring folk.

"But, but… I've never…"

"Sorry, there's not much moss but there be plenty of swaddling," called the Landlady.

'Moss, what? Swaddling?' thought Thomas, climbing the stairs. He was sure he could hear Sir Gladforthe chuckle. It wasn't funny at all.

In a small room with only a tiny window for light, stood a simple table against the wall. A tiny shaft of light shone on the large bowl of water and a couple of piles of rough folded cloths. Thomas wondered if they were meant to be towels. And what was this pile of dry moss for?

Somehow Thomas managed to clean the baby by dipping its bottom in the bowl a bit and wiping away the dark, smelly mess.

"That's the last time I give you bilberries," said Thomas.

"Blurffffpzzzzz… pap, pap, pap," gurgled the baby.

"Yes. Pap! Purple Pap! Indeed," said Thomas, shaking his head while focusing on tying the cloths around the baby. Soon he had done a very good job of wrapping his arm in with the baby and the strips of cloth. The little baby giggled and cooed and pulled at his finger.

"Stop!" said the Landlady, entering the room. "Such a tat of swaddling, baby and boy."

Quickly she took over, untangling Thomas, and then she showed the lad how to look after the baby. At last she packed a sack of spare cloths and swaddling.

"Thank you, my lady," said Thomas.

They shared a smile. Thomas was pleased he now knew what the moss was for. He gazed upon the baby, amazed at how happy she was now that she'd eaten and was in clean cloths.

"Coo… cooo, pap, pap, pap!"

Thomas was growing fond of this little one.

Chapter Twenty-Four
A Promise

Thomas carried the baby outside where Sir Gladforthe was waiting.

"We will make camp here till the Landlady brings news," said the Knight.

The little baby cooed.

"What shall we call her, Sir Gladforthe?"

"This baby is not ours to name. Nay! Why should we think of naming her?"

"No, no! How can we *not* name her?" Thomas argued. "She will be my ward until we find her family. Yes and I will call her Melody. It's a lovely name. It was… it is my… my… someone I know, it's her name…"

"Tis a serious promise, lad… thee are bound by it."

Thomas looked at little baby Melody and frowned a bit. He thought about the basket, the loneliness of the woods, the maybe robbers or bears or wolves and finding the forest fruits. As he looked at this little baby, he could not help but smile.

Little Melody reached up and pulled on his shirt button, blew a raspberry and gurgled, "Pa, pap, pap."

"Yes, I promise. I will look after her." And to his surprise, he kissed the baby on her brow. Why did he do that? He blushed, glancing over to Sir Gladforthe who seemed busy setting up camp behind the Inn.

"I promise," Thomas whispered to baby Melody.

"Tis a fine name for a girl. Melody. Like a chant," said Sir Gladforthe.

Night fell and all were asleep.

Chapter Twenty-Five
Thunder

With a start, Thomas sat up, wide awake in the darkness. As his eyes adjusted, he could make out little Melody by his side, giggling in her sleep. He smiled then searched the darkness for Sir Gladforthe. There he was, sound asleep by the horses.

'All good,' thought Thomas.

He was just about to settle down to sleep again when he heard thunder far across the valley. Was that thunder? He listened. No, it sounded different. Was that a cracking or crackling? He thought he could hear another sound like a wail… or a cry… or birds maybe? Thomas felt uneasy. He picked up his ward, untethered the horses, and was about to wake the Knight, but Sir Gladforthe was already packing up their camp.

"Run over to the Innkeeper," said the Knight, "and tell them to board the doors and have some arms at the ready. Raiders are coming! Quick, lad! Do as I bade!"

Thomas ran across the yard and banged on the Innkeeper's door, shouting, "Raiders! Raiders coming! Get your arms!" he banged again "Raid…"

The upstairs shutters flew open and the Innkeeper peered into the darkness, his wife's shawl draped hastily around his shoulders.

"Then it be true!" shouted the Innkeeper's wife. "They must be after the baby. You must take her into the woods, there's a safe house there! Quickly, remember these words and say them once you enter…

Follow the ash, the oak, the buckthorn, the pine,
the hazel, the hawthorn, keep to the line,
Follow the blackthorn, the oak and the ash,
Into wild wolves. White teeth will gnash."

"What was that? Follow the oak, the hazel, the what?" bellowed Thomas. He could hear the distant noises growing louder. Was that hooves?

"Thomas," called Sir Gladforthe, "we must be swift, as swift as the bird on the wing. The horses are ready."

"Listen carefully," urged the Innkeeper's wife. "Ye must follow the line of the rhyme, do not falter. Ye must follow the rhyme, tree by tree." Then, the Innkeeper and his wife repeated the chant as loud as they could muster and closed the window shutters.

The rhyme rang around in Thomas's head, over and over, as they quickly slipped into the woods by the ash and the oak, the leaves closing behind them.

'That's weird,' thought Thomas. He was very scared now but tried to be brave in case little Melody woke up.

"Wait here, lad," said the Knight. "Ye are quite safe in this magical wood but remember the incantation when I return."

Thomas nodded. He was pretty sure that incantation meant the Innkeepers' magical rhyme.

Sir Gladforthe slipped back out through the leaves and crept close to the goat pen, keeping to the shadows.

Chapter Twenty-Six
Search Party

Soon, Thomas, hidden by leaves and branches, watched the raiders gallop up to the Inn, swords shining in the light of their fiery torches. Thomas recognised the horsemen as those he saw in the woods!

One of the unarmoured men jumped from his horse and banged on the Inn door with the hilt of his crude sword. No answer. He banged again and shouted, "Innkeeper! Open this door in the King's name!"

'So they're not robbers…' thought Thomas.

The Innkeeper's wife opened the top window slowly and peered out. Behind the front door the Innkeeper waited, ready, club in hand.

"Dear me," she yawned, looking very sleepy in her nightgown and shawl. "What can the King's men be wanting at this hour? Food, is it? I've some hog roast from last week you are welcome to, it could be a bit mealy now though, thinking on, but the bread was fresh yesterday."

Thomas was sure she was stalling.

"SILENCE, WENCH!" bellowed the armoured Knight. "There is talk of a baby, a young boy and a Sir Knight stopped here for vitals."

"Yes, that be true," replied the Innkeeper's wife. "The boy and a baby were escorted by a Knight."

"When and where did they go?" demanded the armoured Knight.

"Ooh, let's see… they must have left early evening and headed down the road."

"You lie, wench! We would have seen them. Now tell me, where did they go? I have the King's word that I can use any means to get to the truth!"

A soldier leaned down from his horse holding a burning torch close to the thatch of the goat's pen.

Sir Gladforthe quickly withdrew deeper into the shadows.

"Sire, sire, have mercy please!" cried the Innkeeper's wife. "They told me that's where they were going, but I didn't see which way as I was serving food and drink inside. We were proper busy. I was bumping from table to kitchen and piles of washing up in the trough. No, I didn't see which way. I did not have time, Sire."

The armoured Knight signalled to the soldier. "See if you can pick up their trail." Then turning to the Innkeeper's wife, he said, "But, if you lie, wench… ye will pay."

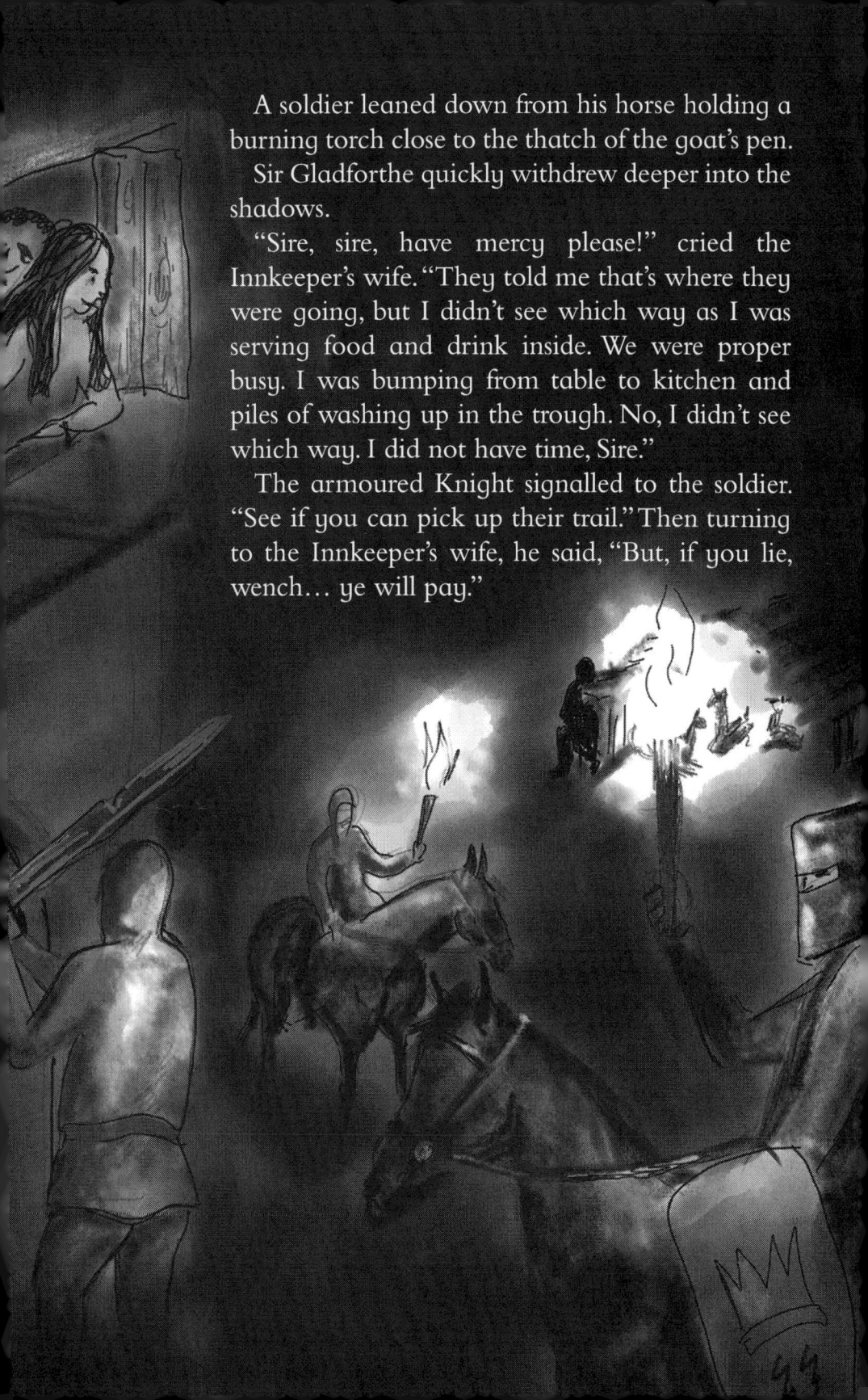

Chapter Twenty-Seven
Silly King

Silently, Sir Gladforthe crept towards Thomas who quickly whispered...

> "Follow the ash, the oak, the buckthorn, the pine,
> the hazel, the hawthorn, keep to the line,
> Follow the blackthorn, the oak and the ash,
> Into wild wolves. White teeth will gnash."

The leaves parted then seemed to swallow them up, carrying them swiftly deeper and deeper into the dense dark forest. There was barely a sound when they stopped.

"What is happening? Where are we? Why does the King want my Melody?" asked Thomas.

"Tis said that a new queen is born under the stars. She will bring great fortune, peace and wisdom beyond measure to the land. The King wants his own son to take the throne, but the people do not wish it, for he is cruel and hath not the grace of his father."

"But why do they want Melody?" Thomas demanded, clutching the baby.

"When she is but twelve years old, the King will force baby Melody to marry the prince!"

"What at twelve years old? That's just silly! Children can't get married," Thomas laughed, shaking his head. "Unbelievable! What a silly king!"

"Then we agree," smiled Sir Gladforthe.

Chapter Twenty-Eight
"I've picked up their trail, Sire."

"Into the woods, lads! They can't be far away!"

The soldiers entered the woods. Following the trail, they passed by the blackthorn and the oak, and were soon deep within the forest, its soft leafy floor deadening the sounds of hoof and clanking armour. They stopped by an ash tree.

"We've lost the trail, Sire."

"Silence! I can hear them. Hold your horses," said the King's Knight.

All around them, they could hear footsteps and then... growling.

"Sire...? I don't think that be a boy, a baby or a Knight. It be wolves." whimpered one soldier.

They glanced about trying to place the growls, only just making out the flashes of grey fur and bared teeth that leapt around the soldier's horses. A wolf howled nearby. The horses reared up onto their hind legs, startled, eyes wild and snorting through flared nostrils. They bolted in different directions.

Not one rider could steer their steed for the wolves' teeth were snapping at each horse's hooves. On and on the horses galloped, their riders barely hanging on, bouncing and clanking in their saddles as the wolves gave chase. Strangely, no sooner were the horses and their riders out of the forest, the wolves seemed to vanish in the bright daylight.

After a while, once the horses were settled, the King's men each agreed that they must head back to the Palace with haste to tell the King how brave they were. The wolves were very scared, weren't they?

"Probably eaten by wolves." suggested the King's Knight. "We will tell his Majesty as much. The princess is surely gone. Alas."

"Yes, Sire. Eaten by wolves, alas."

43

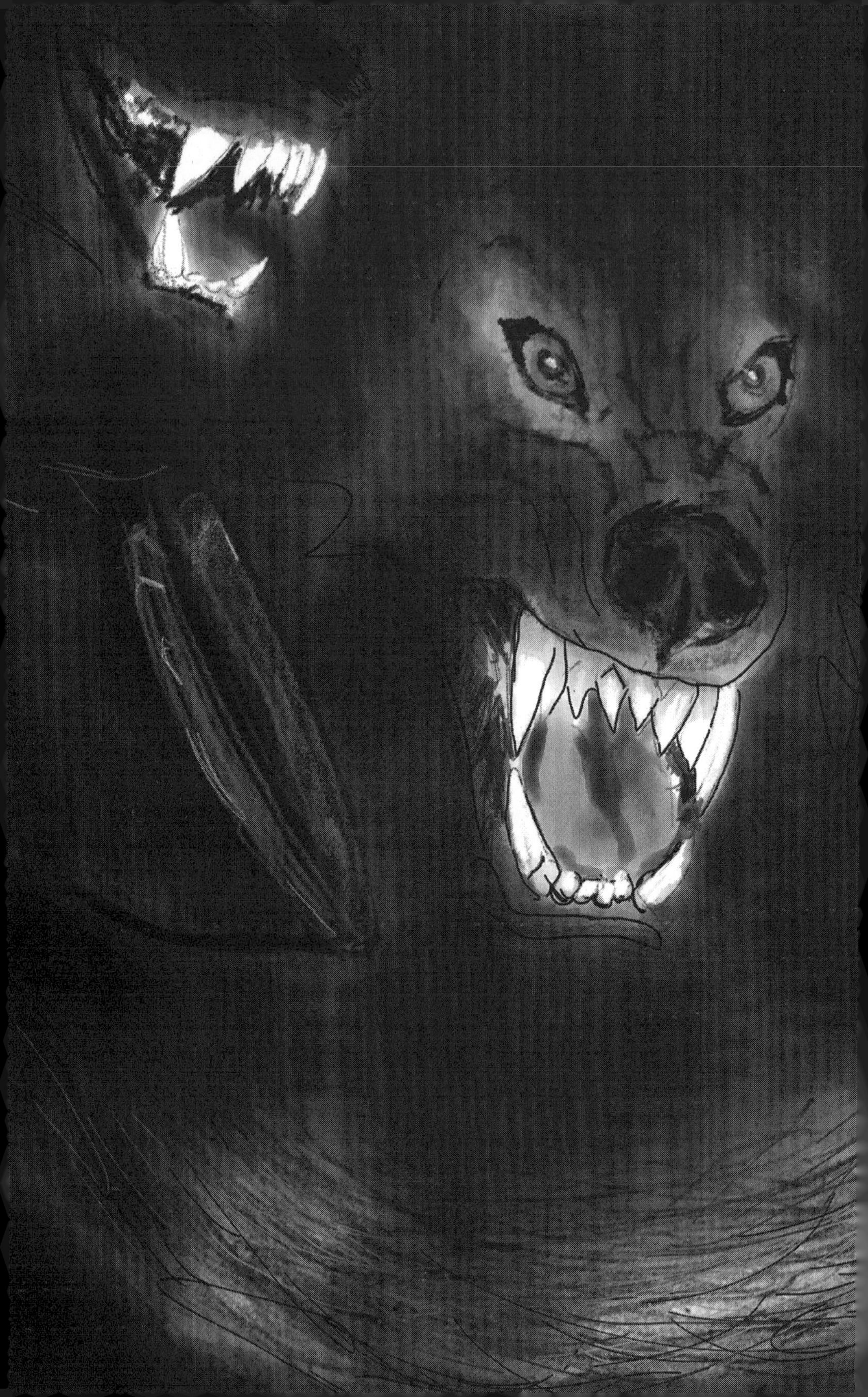

Chapter Twenty-Nine
What is a Which?

The little family made their way through the forest following the path with "The Ash, the Oak, the Buckthorn, the Pine" trees. What little light there had been seemed to be fading. Had they been riding all day? Ahead of them at the end of the path was a cave entrance. A warm light shone from within. As they approached, a tall lady emerged in front of the cave.

"What is this? Which are thee?" she said. "What is which's future, the other which place to be?"

"Dear lady," Sir Gladforthe began. "May I present..."

"The true heir to the throne born under the stars," said the lady.

"Yes, I believe so, m'lady," the Knight continued, "and this is..."

"The What that is a Which," said the lady.

Thomas felt a warm wet on his arm. He glanced down at Melody, who looked like she did before the blueberry stink! He piped up, "Melody needs a new nappy, Sire!"

"Bring her inside, What," said the lady. "I have everything prepared."

"What?" said Thomas.

"Ye. Yes, ye. What, come in. Ye too, Knight," said the lady.

Thomas looked quizzically at Sir Gladforthe, who nodded. They dismounted and entered the cave. To Thomas's surprise, the cave was just like Granddad's living room and there, on a blue and pink chair, sat the tall lady.

"Change the baby over there, What," she said. "There is all you need."

"Why do you keeping saying what?" said Thomas. He was getting grumpy now.

"Thomas," warned the Knight. "Forgive my ward, m'lady, he is concerned for the baby."

"Ye," said the lady, pointing to Thomas. "Ye… you are the what that is a which."

Thomas still didn't understand, but because the baby was getting a bit twisty, he decided to change her first. 'Aww, she's probably tired and hungry,' thought Thomas as he cooed and kissed her forehead. On the table was a bowl of water, cotton wool and a modern nappy, not cloths, dried moss or swaddling cloth.

"Waa waa!" cried baby Melody, as Thomas changed her much quicker and much easier than before!

Chapter Thirty
The Un-muddling

"Now then, boy, come hither," said the lady.

Thomas noticed that she was knitting something he had seen somewhere before, and this woman was sitting on his... his...

"What is the What you seek? What is it you seek, boy?"

"Well, Sir Gladforthe said I am under the spell of Muddled Memory," Thomas began.

"Now, you have memory, you say, but it is muddled. Tis not your memory you seek but it's un-muddling."

"Oh I see," said Thomas. But he did not.

"But why is your memory muddled like a tat of tangled wool?" She smiled gently at Thomas. "What is hidden at the inner end of this muddle of woolly memory?"

"I do not know," said Thomas, but as he spoke, he knew his words didn't ring true although he hadn't meant to lie.

"You do." She held his gaze. "A boy has the answer but it is stuck. He does not want to look."

"Why does she speak in rhyme all the time?" Thomas whispered to Sir Gladforthe at his side. But Sir Gladforthe simply pushed him gently towards the wise tall lady.

"There is something you do not wish to remember," she said. "Now, which is the what? What, tell me?"

"No, there's not!" declared Thomas, folding his arms. But he knew she was right... he didn't want to remember.

The wise lady held him in her gaze for some time, swaying her head slowly from side to side, smiling. Then she handed him a load of brown muddy coloured wool.

"Here un-tat this messy bundle, there is magic inside," she said gently.

Thomas was a bit unsure why he had to sit untangling the wool, but nevertheless did just that. He knew it was going to

Secret

take ages. As he sat there, he glanced up at the tall lady and in that moment he thought he recognised her, a rush of tears welled up.

"Grandma! My Nana! Nana!" he cried.

The tall lady took his hands in hers and Thomas collapsed into her arms where he cried and sobbed. His whole body shook as he told her why he'd run and run, and how he'd not stopped until he couldn't think.

He told her of his quest, the Knight, swimming, robbers, fishing, oaths, spells and they all laughed about the Princess's pongy nappies. Finally he told her all about his marvellous Nana, the custard she'd always burnt, the bike rides, the pictures and all the cuddles. He would miss her forever.

As he was talking through his adventures, he remembered his knitted knight. He looked down for his toy. But in his hand was a piece of wool, not a knight. He had never ever been without his toy that his Nana had made… with love, for him. He felt the ache in his heart, a pain that said, "I miss you, Grandma!" He still hurt but his heart was soft, the stone had melted.

Thomas looked up at Sir Gladforthe and said, "My Mum and Dad will be wondering where I am. Will you take me back, Sir Gladforthe?"

The lady answered. "They will be here soon. Pull on the wool in your hand, quickly now. Goodbye… for now."

Thomas did as he was bade and began pulling.

"Remember to make it into a ball like your Grandma taught ye." said the lady.

Wrapping the wool round and round one way then the other, on he pulled until Sir Gladforthe's boot began to unravel. The first thing he saw was a pair of blue slippers just like Granddad's. He kept pulling and winding. 'Those look a bit like Granddad's jeans,' thought Thomas, and his jumper. Underneath the gloves were his Granddad's hands. On the wrist, his Granddad's old watch with the scratched glass face. Finally as he unwound the helmet, there was his Granddad… his beard and glasses.

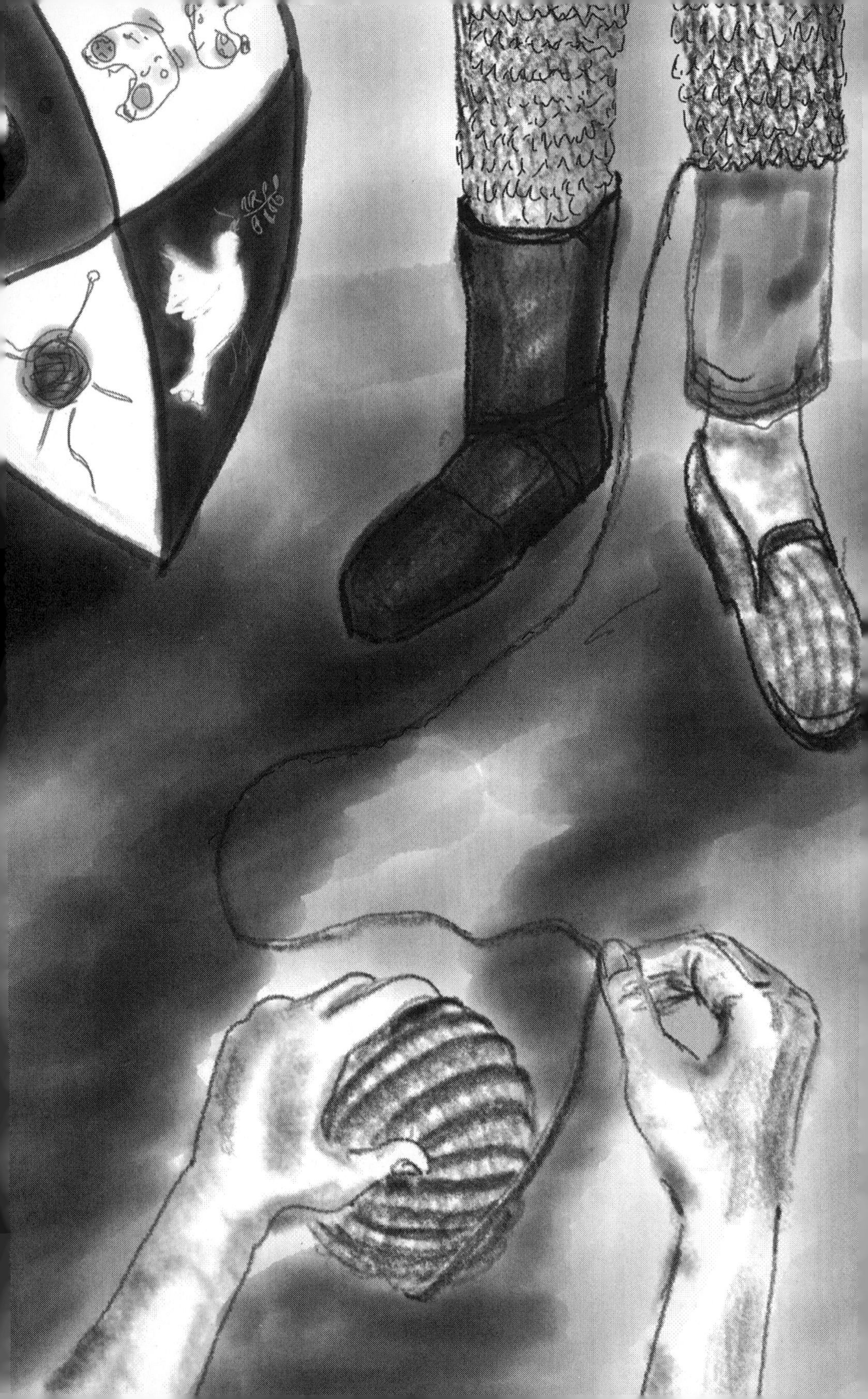

Chapter Thirty-One
Home

"Granddad! It's you!" said Thomas.

"Thomas!" cried Granddad. "You're back! I've been here all along."

"Yes, I know," said Thomas. "You were with me on the quest."

"A quest, eh?" said Granddad. "What que…"

DING-DONG! The doorbell rang.

"Ah. That'll be your Mum and Dad…"

Granddad opened the door. "He's come back to us."

His Mum and Dad rushed past Granddad to greet their lovely little boy.

"Thomas!" said his Mum. "We've been so worried about you. You've been…"

"On a quest with his Knight," said Granddad.

Thomas looked at his Granddad, his parents and his knitted knight. Sharing a smile with his Granddad, he said, "Sir Gladforthe has been looking after me."

"Oh, I see," said his Mum but she didn't really. "That's good then. Well, we'd better introduce you to your new baby sister, she's called…"

"Melody," said Thomas.

His parents opened their mouths in silent disbelief, then watched speechless as Thomas jumped out of bed and kissed little Melody on the forehead.

"She's a little Princess," he said.

Melody smiled and cooed. "Pap, pap, pap."

'She knows,' thought Thomas.

That evening, Thomas crept into his new baby sister's bedroom. Melody looked ever so sweet, even when she pumped. He knew he would look after her forever… but he would never ever feed her bilberries.

Thomas remembered the words of the Master of the Woods...
"And Sir Gladforthe, when you are done, there is a new position you must take, without question."

Thomas looked at his knitted knight and said, "This is your new ward, Melody." Then he placed his beloved knitted toy at the bottom of his baby sister's cradle.

"This is Sir Gladforthe," he told Melody. "He's your knitted knight now. He'll look after you too. Your Grandma made him with all her love. Her name was Melody too. She couldn't finish your toy before she left, so you can have mine. She'd like that. Don't tell Mum and Dad that Sir Gladforthe is magic."

"Ga goo ga goo ga? Pap pap pap."

"Night night, little sis," said Thomas. "Sleep tight."

The end.